2012 PRESIDENTIAL ADDRESS

'BY BUS AND BOAT ON BR'

given by

COLIN PAGE

To a meeting of the Society at
The Cube,
Moor Street Station,
Birmingham,
on 13th October 2012,

subsequently repeated at
London Road Station,
Brighton,
on 13th April 2013,

and again at
The Friends Meeting House,
Mount Street,
Manchester,
on 8th June 2013

The Transport Ticket Society
2014

*The production of this publication has also been made possible thanks
to the bequest to the Society by the late Courtney Haydon
who was a member for about 34 years*

*Further copies of this and other Publications may be obtained from the
Society's Publication Sales Officer:*

Steve Skeavington
6 Breckbank,
Forest Town,
MANSFIELD.
NG19 0PZ

*Comments etc. regarding this publication are welcome;
please write to the Hon. Secretary,*

Alan Peachey
4 The Sycamores,
BISHOPS STORTFORD.
CM23 5JR

Published by

The Transport Ticket Society
4 The Sycamores,
Bishops Stortford.
CM23 5JR

© Colin Page 2014

ISBN 978-0-903209-79-3

Printed by

Prontaprint Brighton & Hove
190 Church Road
Hove
BN3 2DJ

Introduction

The genesis for this address has its beginnings in a boat trip I made as a young lad in the early 1960's. I had already been collecting tickets for a number of years – well before I was able to join the TTS - when I obtained a ticket which was entirely unexpected in its style and format for the journey I was about to make.

It was issued by British Railways as a railway ticket, which I thought was very strange since I was on a boat. As a result of this find I began to collect tickets from a similar background as a special interest in themselves. The common feature is that the ticket itself is issued by British Railways but is for a journey which does not involve travel by rail, at the very least for the first part of the trip, or is issued by BR for use on foreign railway services.

As the years passed this collection grew, based around the mid 1960's but covering the period from the beginning of BR through to the 1970's. Eventually I decided that one way of making it of more interest was to look at the operations of British Railways which did not involve railways and then go and search for tickets. So I have organised this address by effectively selecting all the appropriate routes and operations and then examining each of them on a geographical basis.

I decided to talk about my special interest in these tickets as a result of the need to give an Address to my fellow members which came about when I was elected as President in 2012. In order to make the talk manageable I have selected only a couple of representative specimens from each location although I point out that there are considerably more tickets than are referred to and there are many more that I do not possess. I have also extended the address to include other forms of transport and related subjects which British Railways operated but in which there is no standard gauge rail interest. British Railways running buses and toll bridges? Surely not.

The histories of the places and activities we visit are more than adequately covered in the extensive bibliography now available of the ships and buses we encounter and I have not included such details within the following text, except for the occasional date which seems pertinent. In particular all the shipping and bus activities visited were inherited by BR in 1948 and thus I shall list only closure dates where relevant, or opening dates for newer activities. A feature that has become very apparent when I gave the addresses was that we could have dropped anchor at many of the ports or got off at bus stations to discuss individual tickets, such is the amount of information printed on them. This is even more appropriate when I acknowledge the very extensive database of information that we have within the Society contained in the pages of *Journal* and published documents. I have therefore decided to adopt the principle that the tickets can 'talk for themselves' and I only add details where a particular item needs further attention.

I was allowed to join the Society "under age" in 1965 as by then I had amassed a collection in size which was considered and deemed suitable for me to become a member. I've been a member ever since. Incidentally, my interest in water goes back to when I was an even smaller lad, as I attempted to divert rivers flowing out of rock pools on the beach wherever we were on holiday. My interest became part of my career when I spent my professional working life in clean water and sewage, designing and constructing treatment works.

I would like to thank the many members of the Society who I have now known over many, many years for their friendship and support. I have always found it a great pleasure to come across fellow members unexpectedly at a railway station or airport or in the middle of nowhere, all of us on travels far and wide, and pursuing the current ticketing arrangements. Similarly it is always good fun to meet for an afternoon to talk about tickets.

I especially want to thank my two life-long pals for their particular involvement in this endeavour. Phil Drake, for provision of choice specimens from his collection, which are included in this address, and to Roger Overin for formatting the publication.

By Bus and Boat on BR

I have this vision of the new Chairman of the British Transport Commission, Sir Cyril Hurcomb, Railway Executive, on 1st January 1948, reviewing his assets. "Several thousand steam locos, some electrical machines, a couple of new-fangled diesels (they won`t last long) and – what`s this Carruthers? Some ships? Which stations do they sail from? I don`t know Sir.  And some buses. Where`s Yorkshire? Mmmm. I think we`ll put those to one side for the moment".

And there they were left, especially the ships, seemingly forgotten, until the early 1960's when it became apparent that they needed replacement. The travel market was by now very different from that of 15 years previously, particularly with the growing impact of the car and the need to ferry these as rolling rather than deck cargo.

So where shall I start my voyage of exploration?

This is a Derby trolleybus.

<1>

Please do not worry, trolleybuses do not feature in the address but I have had a real interest in these vehicles since the early 1960's so I could not resist the opportunity to include one here. But it's the advertisement that I am interested in. "Drinka Pinta Milka Day". What is this all about? Questions were asked in the House. "We can`t have the Queen`s English messed about like this". However such phraseology is now commonplace and the marketing folk at BR were quick to latch onto such language when they were promoting the latest ferry services across the Irish Sea. "StranHeyHolyFish" says the brochure <2> .

I first saw this on a hoarding on the Stratford Road (the A34 about 3 miles south of our location here at Moor Street Station). At the time I had no idea what it was to do with but of course it depicts the initial syllables of the four mainland ports for ferries to Ireland, namely Stranraer, Heysham, Holyhead and Fishguard, all owned and operated by British Railways at the time.

<2>

<1> The trolleybus is Derby Corporation 207, a Sunbeam F4 with Brush H30/26R body, built in 1948 and shown at the Allen Street turning circle short working on route 60 to Shelton Lock.

Photograph by P J Thomas, picture 96, featured in "Derby Trolleybuses, Trolleybus Classics No 7" and included by kind permission of Middleton Press, tel 01730 813169.

<2> Included with kind acknowledgement to the collection of Bjorn Larssen.

StranHeyHolyFish

Stranraer to Larne

<3>

<4>

<5>

<6>

Let's go to Stranraer (Harbour) and buy a single to Larne (Harbour) <3> and <4>. We are given a ticket exactly of the type I am intrigued by. It is a standard railway Edmondson but for a journey which involves no rail travel. There is nothing on the ticket to indicate this. Moreover, there is no reference either, in the conditions on the reverse, to any nautical activity <5> and <6>. If we examine the conditions in some detail then I believe we have an answer as to why this is the case. Illustration <7> shows an extract from the "BTC British Railways Extracts from the Book of Regulations containing Conditions of Carriage of Passengers &c" – specifically "Condition of issue of tickets available by Water &c… (Regulation 16)" dated 1st July 1958 which clearly shows that for the purposes of administration all shipping activities are classed as railway activities. Hence, on all the tickets which I will now show, except with one or two specimens, there is no reference to them being for a journey across water and without a rail journey being involved, or at least on the first part of the journey. It was this feature that fascinated me with that ticket I mentioned at the beginning and which I will illustrate at the end.

CONDITIONS OF ISSUE OF TICKETS AVAILABLE BY WATER AND
REGULATIONS AND CONDITIONS APPLICABLE TO CARRIAGE
OF ACCOMPANIED LUGGAGE BY WATER.

(Regulation 16.)

All the foregoing Regulations and Conditions shall, in so far as they are capable of being applied, apply to the carriage of passengers and their luggage and property in the Commission's vessels, and for this purpose the expression "train" shall include "vessels" and notwithstanding the provisions of Definition (iii), Page 3, the expressions "station", "platform" and "junction" shall include any "port", "pier", "dock", "wharf", and "landing stage" at which the Commission's vessels embark or disembark passengers and their accompanied luggage, and the expression "guard's van", "luggage van" and "luggage vehicle" shall include any "luggage hold" or "luggage room" or "strong room" in a vessel.

The carriage of passengers and their luggage in the Commission's vessels is also subject to the following special Conditions and in the case of inconsistency between such Conditions and the foregoing Regulations and Conditions, the following special Conditions shall prevail:—

(1) The Commission and their servants and agents shall be exempt from all liability for injury (fatal or otherwise), loss, damage or delay in respect of the passenger himself arising from any act, neglect or default whatsoever in the management or navigation of any vessel during the voyage of such vessel or at or during the loading or discharging or the arrival or departure thereof.

The Commission in making this Condition do so for themselves and for and on behalf of each and every one of their servants or agents and the acceptance of the ticket by the passenger shall be conclusive evidence of his agreement that in the event of any injury (fatal or otherwise), loss,

<7>

It could be argued that there is some logic to this when perhaps the ships and ports are seen as being assets. Indeed when TOPS (Total Operations Processing System) was introduced in 1974 the class number 99 was given to fourteen ships (as 99001 to 99014) in the Sealink fleet which were capable of carrying railway rolling stock and were classed as train ferries. These sailed to the Continent.

Also, to put all of this into some historical context, a brief outline of what happened to the ships and buses around this time is useful. After its formation on 1st January 1948 the Railway Executive was abolished on 30th September 1953 and became the British Transport Commission. This then became the British Railways Board in 1963 and rebranded its trading name of British Railways into British Rail in 1965 when new corporate colours and the double arrow logo were introduced. The shipping interests were separated in 1968 into a new division and in 1970 a new marketing name of Sealink was introduced. Then in 1978 ownership of the vessels was transferred to Sealink UK Ltd as a wholly owned subsidiary and as a prelude to privatisation of the railways. Sealink was then acquired on 27th July 1984 by Sea Containers Ltd for £66m and became Sealink British Ferries (SBF). Stena Line then completed a hostile takeover of SBF in 1990 after a lengthy battle and operated as Stena Sealink Line until being absorbed into the main Stena Line fleet a few years later. As an additional aid to dating tickets 3rd class was abolished on 3rd June 1956. The differentiation between 1st and 2nd class on board ships was abolished on 5th January 1970.

The circumstances of ownership by BR of buses in Yorkshire is complicated and well documented but an easy end/way out of their involvement is that BR passed ownership of their buses to the National Bus Company on 1st January 1969 and which were then subsumed into the formation of the PTEs in 1969 South Yorkshire Passenger Transport Executive (SYPTE) and 1974 West Yorkshire Passenger Transport Executive (WYPTE).

Having digressed we return to Stranraer, <8>, <9>, <10>, <13>.

Managing passengers onto and off the ships required the special type of ticket entitled "Control Ticket". Many travel tickets had extended validity which in the case of returns only stipulated the period within which the return could be made. So in order to keep track of the number of spaces available on a particular sailing Control Tickets to this number were issued which passengers had to obtain at the time of their desired crossing <11>, <14>. Of particular interest is ticket 0122 <11> where reference is made on the reverse to water, despite comments so far <12>.

<8>

<9>   <10>

<11>   <12>

<13>   <14>

7353 <15> mentions Stranraer to Larne as the relevant crossing but is for a British Railways agency issue starting in Northern Ireland. It makes no mention of how the holder actually gets from Belfast to Larne least of all that it is not British Railways who is the operator.

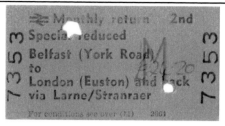

<15>

Heysham to Belfast

Here are tickets <16>, <17> from Heysham (Harbour) to Belfast and a ticket for a similar journey in the opposite direction.

Note the anonymity of the location of tickets as just Belfast. This is a common feature of these tickets as will be depicted in later tickets. I am not sure how the passenger is expected to know the location of the pier (Donegall Quay) but perhaps it is because it is obvious.

<16>

<17>

<18>

Another type of ticket is now depicted for the berths allocated to passengers on board. The two shown here <18>, <19>, respectively for 1st and 2nd class are both bi-directional. <20> introduces a variation of control ticket, here entitled "Regulated Sailing Ticket" but which is printed on thin card (normal paper as referenced to Ultimate tickets) presumably because it would be cheaper than printing Edmondsons.

<19>

<20>

<21> and <22> illustrate tickets issued from a Westinghouse Handiprinter mark II machine. About 250 of these were allocated to stations throughout the London Midland Region and a few on the Western Region main line from Paddington from the very early 1970's until the arrival of APTIS in 1986, but it is particularly interesting that BR should consider them worthy enough for several machines to be allocated to ports and offices in Ireland. It is conceivable that the Handiprinter was seen as an ideal machine where the inherent flexibility of being able to issue any ticket from anywhere to anywhere else would be very beneficial, especially when only small quantities of a particular route were needed. Incidentally, these machine nos., numbers 01B and 02B both allocated to the BR pier office in Belfast, were numerically the first of the mark II machines and were also amongst the very first to be put into use in 1970. Note that 8513, <21>, is issued against a Forces Duty warrant (so no fare was paid) in 1970, at the beginning of "The Troubles".

<21>

<22>

Of the four Irish sea ferries this was the least used. Closure was announced in 1974 and the ferry service was withdrawn on 5th April 1975, when the Donegall Quay ticket office closed. At this time, bookings from the Heysham Harbour office had been met with Edmondsons, although a Handiprinter (77D) was located for rail bookings until this station closed on 6th October 1975.

Holyhead to Dun Laoghaire

The principle route to Ireland was (and remains) via Holyhead . The BR ferry port in Ireland was at Dun Laoghaire and illustrated <23>, <24> and <25> are a selection of tickets for this journey, all showing the features now established by the earlier tickets. Ticket 2811, <23> is from Handiprinter mk II machine 94D located at Holyhead. The journey is in fact for the return sector from Dun Laoghaire. This is determined because the ticket shown is the return half, as return tickets printed by Handiprinters were in two identical halves except for OUT and RTN as shown at the bottom. <26> depicts an excess ticket for an upgrade to first class for a passenger holding a ticket otherwise for second class. <27> is probably a printers proof but I have not been able to find out any significance of the date.

<23>

<24>

<25>

<26>

<27>

<28> is a similar control ticket to **<20>** and the two are compared below. Both have the same form number.

<28>

<20>

Dublin (Westland Row)   is better known today as Pearse, being renamed in 1966, and is a station on the DART network. But in the days of this address it was the main station on the south of the Liffey and on the direct line to Dun Laoghaire and Rosslare, so would be an obvious point for BR tickets to be available to for Irish Sea crossings, although not as stock. This ticket is an agency issue from I believe the Sealink office in London Victoria (971). **<29>**.

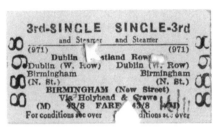

<29>

British Railways did have an office in Dublin, located in Westmoreland St, which is the   extension of O'Connell St to the south of the Liffey. The presence of a Handiprinter machine (ticket 9949) is fascinating **<30>** and as with the Belfast issues, it must have been determined that they could usefully be located there as well. Depicted is a ticket from mk II machine number 46D.   Five different Handiprinters were allocated from the late 1970's to Westmoreland St and three to Dun Laoghaire although not necessarily at the same time. **<31>** depicts Dun Laoghaire (K. Pier).   The town was named Kingstown between 1821 and 1920.   The appendage Kingstown Pier was continued into the 1960's and was dropped in 1966 when the current station became just Dun Laoghaire.

<31>

<30>

Outside the dates of this address but included is a spread of very recent Fujitsu tickets to show that it is still possible to obtain tickets for just the water part of the journey <32>, <33>, <34> and <35>. "Dublin FYPT I F" translates as Dublin Ferryport, Irish Ferries.

<32>

<33>

<34>

<35>

When relocating from Holyhead to Fishguard along the Cambrian coastline it is necessary to cross the bridge at Barmouth where BR finds itself at this time administering the toll. The ticket illustrated <36> may at first seem rather mundane but raises a few points and questions. Who was the printer, clearly not one of the common ones? Having the pair reveals that they are printed 'upside down' when compared with usual punch tickets, as the number is at the bottom and upside down. Quite possibly they could have been printed by a local firm, and Mr Speake would thereby ensure he had his name on them. Gwynedd Council took over management of the toll in 1975 but it lapsed in April 2013 when the couple who acted on behalf of the Council to collect the tolls were made redundant.

<36>

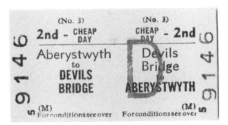

<37>

Just as we thought we were in reach of Fishguard we find another form of transport that BR owned, namely the Vale of Rheidol (VoR) narrow gauge railway at Aberystwyth, one of whose claims to fame is that it became the last outpost of steam traction owned by BR when mainline steam ceased in August 1968. The tickets themselves from the period in question are of usual BR format and type and a selection that could be obtained then are depicted. The booking office for the VoR at the time was separate from the mainline office and this is reflected in the tickets (no3 as shown on 9146). <37>, <38>, <39> and <40>. The reference number on ticket 1034 confirms that this issue is accounted for at Aberystwyth (4303). However, nothing on them indicates that they are for a special (i.e. narrow gauge steam) form of transport.

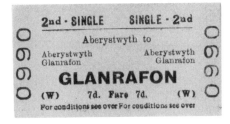

<38>

<39>

<40>

Fishguard to Rosslare (and Waterford)

Fishguard was in the 1960's (and remains) the main port for passage from South Wales and south west England to the south of the Irish Republic, at Rosslare. Foot passengers were the main traffic and were issued with standard BR issues, a pattern that now becomes familiar. Tickets illustrated are typical issues from the period. <41>, <42>, <43>, <44> and <45>.

<41>

<43>

<42>

<44>

<45>

There was another service that BR had inherited from the Great Western Railway (GWR) and which is all but forgotten. It sailed three nights a week to Waterford (Adelphi Quay) and returned a day later. A ticket is illustrated <46> for this service (dated 02 Nov 51). The vessel used was the MV Great Western which sounded grand but was in fact a ship of only 1659 grt, built in 1933. I can imagine that during wild January nights even the Captain would have left the security of either harbour with high trepidation for the ten hour journey across the Irish Sea. The service was withdrawn on 29th June 1959 and lately this quay at Waterford has become developed with riverside flats, with nothing to indicate that steamers once plied the ten miles up the River Suir to dock there <47>. A later issue for the same journey is dated 18 Dec 64 but utilises the Irish rail service from Rosslare to Waterford via Campile <48>.

<46>

<48>

<47>

12

The English Channel to the Dover Strait

Kingswear to Dartmouth

We leave the Principality and head round Lands End where we arrive at the western-most seagoing operation of BR at the time, on the River Dart. A bridge between the railhead at Kingswear and the larger town of Dartmouth on the west bank had been a long held aim but (as I understand) the need for high clearances for shipping to navigate further upstream precluded this. I also believe that awkward geological features in the riverbed prevented the installation of a swing bridge which otherwise would have been the logical type of crossing to build. So the ancient ferry prevailed. When it passed into railway ownership a railway style building was built at Dartmouth, complete with booking office facilities.   Typical issues from the 1960's between the two ports of Dartmouth and Kingswear are illustrated <**49**> and <**50**>. What is noteworthy is that for the first time on our travels a ticket now appears with water-related wording – "ferry". I presume that this is because the ferry is crossing waters which are estuarial i.e. not denoted as "The High Seas" and is therefore subject to different conditions than for ships sailing to foreign lands. Moreover the same fact is seen on the ferry tickets across the Thames and the Humber. I acknowledge that I have been unable to find a reference for this presumption. It would seem logical though for a short and frequent crossing to have some simple form of ticket and this was the case, as paper tickets were indeed issued <**51**>. BR closed the booking office at Dartmouth on 3rd October 1966 and crossing tickets were then issued from Kingswear. Dartmouth station closed on 28th October 1972 and at the end of the year operation of the railway line to Paignton was transferred to the Dart Valley Light Railway Co. The ferry operation was transferred the following day to South Hams Council but was subsequently sold to the DVLR . The ferry still operates in 2012 as a part of the Paignton and Dartmouth Steam Railway.

<49>

<50>

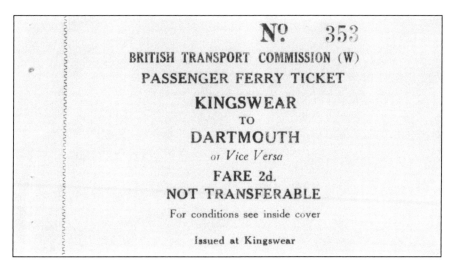

<51>

I approach the BR shipping operations from Weymouth, Portsmouth, Southampton and across the Solent with some trepidation. The history of ferry and shipping services in the area is complicated and not within the scope of this address. I get the impression that even some of the authors of historical books on the subject find the whole matter daunting.

The Channel Islands

The railways served the two Channel Islands of Jersey and Guernsey from early days. Traditionally the ferry services had always sailed from Southampton but with the increasing development of the road network and of the type of vessels themselves changing to roll-on, roll-off configurations the trend seen at some ports was to concentrate traffic on the short sea crossing. The sailings from Southampton to the Channel Islands ceased on 12th May 1961 after which all the main services for passengers and the increasing numbers of cars were then concentrated at Weymouth. Typical issues to Jersey and Guernsey are as illustrated <52>, <53>, <54>, <55>, <56>, together with the attendant control tickets <57>, <58>. Reference 5971 on 5060 <54> and 1456 <53> indicate that these tickets are accounted for at the Jersey office, although the sub mark 00 on 1456 further indicates that this ticket was issued by the Purser. "Q." on 3063 <56> identifies that this ticket was issued from the quay office. Fascinating features of the tickets are the simple designation of the CI ports – Jersey, Guernsey – with no indication of the port, although there was only one such facility on each island.

<52>

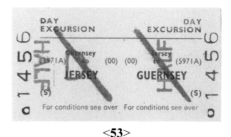

<53>

<54>

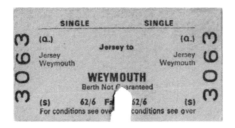

<56>

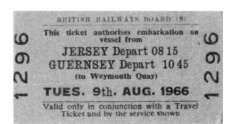

<55>

<57>

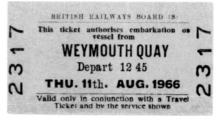

<58>

Ticket <**59**> is interesting in that it is the only example of a ticket that I have in this address which includes the name of the actual ship involved. *Caesarea* was the Roman name for Jersey and her sister ship *Sarnia* carried the Roman name for Guernsey. By many accounts they established a reliable and high level of service across the western approaches to the English Channel. The message on the notice to obtain embarkation tickets <**57**> is both daunting and fascinating. I pity poor Mr Smith having to spend the first hours of his holiday queuing to obtain said tickets, leaving his wife and children to enjoy the seaside delights, and fearful that they could be marooned on the islands indefinitely if he failed to get them. In line with extending operations into other areas and fields, e.g. excursions, with spare capacity created by larger ships, and with quicker turn rounds, it became possible to offer excursions to France and tickets for these are illustrated <**60**>, <**61**>. Note that one is for a non-landing cruise. 0902 on 6698 is a Sealink code.

Ticket <**62**> is issued from a Multiprinter machine but before anyone wonders why Weymouth had such a machine it is in fact issued from Birmingham Snow Hill (machine number 1042) although it is clearly for just the sea crossing of a journey from the inland City to the CIs. It would make sense to have separate tickets for different parts of the trip, especially when different modes were involved and which may well have been individually collected. Moreover the code 26020 is believed to be a dummy reference for accounting purposes (a 'ruse' if you will) to highlight that monies are due to Sealink.

Control Ticket <**63**> is a paper issue from the end period of this address and neatly describes the ownership at this time (1978) of Sealink, as well as depicting that title. Note the poor passenger being advised that there is "no seat available" but is then administered to have an enjoyable journey!

<**59**>

<**60**>

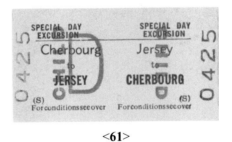

<**61**>

<**62**>

<**63**>

<64>

Meanwhile, some CI operations were transferred to Portsmouth on 8th November 1977 and were subsequently moved to the CFT (= Continental Ferry terminal). Tickets for this are illustrated. <64>, <65>. The Port Tax Ticket <66> reflects that it is Sealink who are operating the service and this is shown on the ticket.

<65>

<66>

Despite these changes, BR maintained a cargo-carrying facility from Southampton to the Channel Islands using the *MV Winchester* on which a dozen berths were available for foot passengers and a paper ticket for a supplementary charge for this is illustrated <67>. The ship was sold in April 1971 to Greek interests and the service was transferred to Portsmouth and then closed as a cargo operation in 1972.

<67>

Southampton

Meanwhile, other passenger carrying ferry services, inherited from the pre-nationalised railway companies, were being operated by BR from Southampton to France and tickets from these operations are illustrated <68>, <69>, <70>, <71>, <72>. The service to Le Havre was withdrawn on 9th May 1964 and that to St Malo on 27th September 1964 which defined the end of such BR sailings from Southampton.

Note that the name 'Havre' is shown without the 'le'. <72>.

Southampton, however, was at this time a principal port for trans Atlantic services and a well organised operation of rail services carried (foot) passengers to and from the dock. Such services have always been referred to as Boat Trains. I cannot find a reason why 'Boat'. Why not Ship train? Keith Farr, in his article in *Railway Magazine* for April 2013 (*) makes no reference to this. For once I will deviate away from the main theme of this address (depicting tickets which do not utilise or start with a railway service) to include illustrations of tickets issued for Boat Trains to and from Southampton <73>, <74>, <75>, <76>, <77>, <78>. They are interesting in themselves as they are relatively late examples of Edmondson cards in use on the network and above all, evoke great memories of the ships involved, all now scrapped or not in service. To assist with dating, Oriana sailed until 1987 whilst M S Astor was launched in 1981 for the Southampton to Cape Town service. Many examples exist for many different ships. Is it possible that BR saw the attraction in providing such special tickets as a memento for the passengers?

(*) Keith Farr, "Boat Trains: Steaming to the Steamers" ; Railway Magazine April 2013

(*) Also - "Ocean Liner Expresses; Boat Trains that ran as required" ; Railway Magazine April 2013.

<68>

<69>

<70>

<71>

<72>

<73>

<74>

<75>

<76>

<77>

<78>

Portsmouth and IOW

BR inherited three ferry services to the Isle of Wight. Portsmouth Harbour to Ryde (foot passengers) and two car ferry services, one from Portsmouth Broad Street to Fishbourne and from Lymington to Yarmouth. Tickets from the era of this address are extensive. These cover, for example, all manner of different vehicle lengths on the car ferry routes and a selection is provided to illustrate the diverse nature of them. During the seventies, the popularity of the car ferry service to Fishbourne progressively outstripped the available terminal facilities at Broad Street, despite 24-hour operation. When Gunwharf power station closed in 1979 Portsmouth City Council bought the land and leased it back to Sealink (still part of BR) who then built a new ferry terminal. On 20th February 1982 the last sailing was made from Broad St slipway and the next day the new terminal at Gunwharf opened. Sadly I do not have any tickets to illustrate for the Fishbourne operation.

Lymington Pier to Yarmouth Slipway <79> to <89>

While the majority of issues for this service are Edmondsons, use was made of Ultimatics for the frequent foot passengers <79>. Note particularly that tickets 1157 <84>, 7121 <85> and 4926 <88>, display the regional code Z which was adopted for BR shipping operations just before privatisation. Also noteworthy for this service is that Edmondsons continued in use after ownership passed to Sealink UK Ltd and for the sake of continuity one of their tickets is illustrated <89>. See also 3612 on <110>. 7121 displays the wording "including VAT and dues". Transport is zero-rated for accounting purposes. Possibly this charge was made very specifically for this category ("One empty commercial vehicle") where expense reimbursement could be involved but this is conjecture.

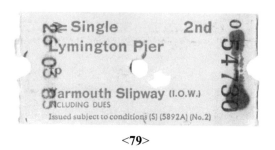

<79>

<80>

<81>

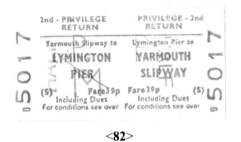

<82>

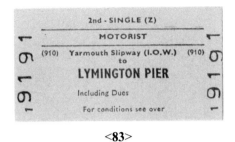

<83>

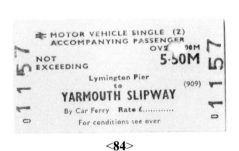

<84>

<85>

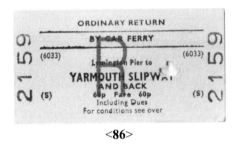

<86>

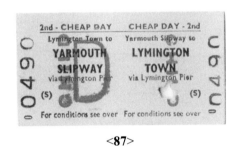

<87>

<88>

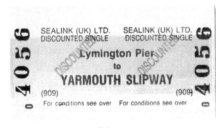

<89>

Portsmouth Harbour to Ryde Pier

BR operated the railway along the pier to the Esplanade. Pedestrians had to pay a toll and four different types of ticket are illustrated for this facility. <90>, <91>, <92>, <93>. 4232 <92> is from an AA machine, commonly used for issuing platform tickets. 79858 <93> is from a Rapidprinter, commonly used at stations for issuing high usage tickets of repetitive journeys.

<90>   <91>

<92>   <93>

A selection of tickets from the period for the ferry service from Portsmouth Harbour to Ryde is illustrated thus <94>, <95>, <96>, <97>. 0348 <94> in effect only gives the holder entitlement to get off at the pier. He then has the choice of travelling on the tram, or the train or walking – for which he would receive a toll ticket as above. 8610 <96> and 4661 <97> are tickets issued from the NCR 21 machine which was used across the Southern Region in the seventies and eighties until the APTIS era of 1986. That from Ryde Esplanade is (so far as I am aware) the only location for one of these machines away from the mainland.

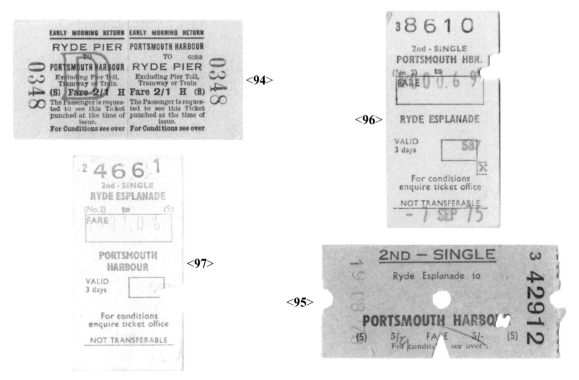

<94>

<96>

<97>

<95>

Newhaven to Dieppe

At Newhaven, the River Ouse provides the only location for a deep water port between Southampton and Dover, which ensured that a ferry to Dieppe could be maintained but the present (2012) very limited demand means the future of the service is perilous. However, back in the 60's a daily service was provided by BR and typical tickets are shown thus <98>, <99>.

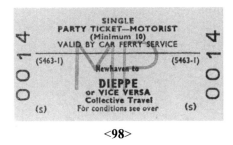

<98>

<99>

At this point I introduce the format of the large paper-type ticket which was in common use at this time for cross-channel bookings. <100> is typical. IC is short for International Coupon. The following number is the UIC code. Here, 87 indicates that SNCF are the issuing authority. 70 represents British Railways (and also Inter-Rail and NIR). The date was often stamped in dot matrix style <101>, as a security measure.

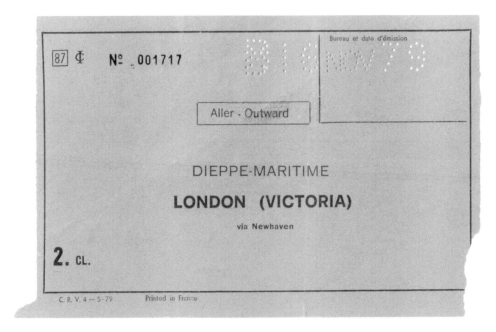

<100>

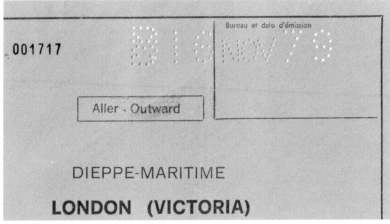

<101>

These tickets were largely superseded by the airline style of ticket which was introduced by BR in the late 1960s, and which became common throughout the network during the 1970s, when operations were now being managed by Sealink. Included is an illustration of this format for this particular crossing. <102> & <103>. We must not overlook that this is technology which prevailed over forty years ago, before the age of computer-issued ticketing. At the time it met the new demands of a universal ticket facility (thereby eliminating preprinted ticket stocks, particularly Edmondsons) and with inbuilt flexibility to cater for all the many and diverse routes and facilities which still existed in BR`s operations and to manage the differing cars and passengers accordingly, which were now becoming normal with roll-on, roll-off ferries. The house style of the tickets evolved as time passed and came to a natural end with the demise of BR-owned Sealink in 1984.

<102>

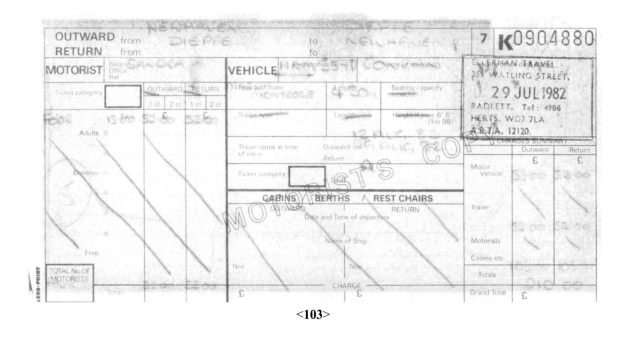

<103>

Straits of Dover

The tickets for the ferries from the cross-channel ports from Folkestone and Dover to Boulogne, Calais, Dunkerque and Oostende can form a whole story in themselves. I am therefore illustrating merely a selection of these <104> to <114>. <104> to <106> are in Southern Railway style as merely copied by BTC after 1948. 0353 <106> shows the port of departure as Dover Marine and the actual quay/station is defined by WO = West Office, where the four-platformed station for foot passengers was located. The tickets in BTC and later BRB style <107> to <110> are agency issues and could perhaps be issued in conjunction with the `main` journey tickets just mentioned, but that is conjecture.

<104>

<105>

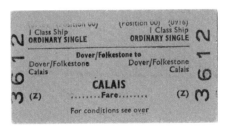

<106>

<107>

<108>

<109>

<110>

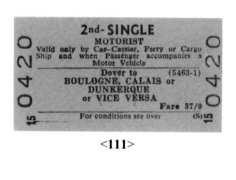

<111>

<112>

<113>

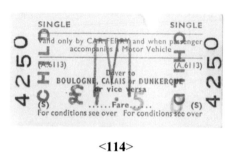

<114>

I do not have any airline style tickets just for the crossing itself and I suspect that this is because most folk were travelling from somewhere else in England to somewhere else on the continent and for which multi-coupon tickets would be issued <115> to <122>. Incidentally, it was this style of ticket that I imagined I would be issued with for my initial water trip (which was an Edmondson). So when I began to find tickets for this particular crossing it was something of a revelation to obtain Edmondsons.

Apart from being bi-lingual, the multi-coupon issues contain a wealth of data and numbers. In particular to be noted are the UIC numbers.

Many of these tickets have a feature which has hitherto not been shown on tickets and that is the inclusion of a pictogram of a ship, perhaps at last providing recognition that these are not in some cases for just railway journeys! <115>, <118>/<120>. The tear-off coupon of ticket 4666 is enlarged to highlight, for the first time, the word 'Boat' <119>.

On <123> is illustrated a landing ticket, clearly defining within the wording what its purpose is. It lays claim to being one of the first water-related tickets I obtained, when I crossed from Dover to Calais on a school trip to Paris in 1964. Somehow I had 'mislaid' it when my time came to disembark.

The ticket illustrated on <124> is configured to enable any combination of the crossings between the ports across the Straits of Dover to be validated and judging by its date (1981) can be considered as a universal facility which must have superseded Edmondsons at agency offices. UIC number 70.

<125> features the three operators on the Dover /Folkestone to Oostende service of which Sealink was a part and incorporates three languages.

<126> recognises that the piers were not just for use of passengers and here we see a paper ticket for admission to Folkestone Pier, presumably for use by fishermen.

Altogether, the Straits of Dover selection provide a fascinating group of tickets within themselves and they form a revered part of my collection.

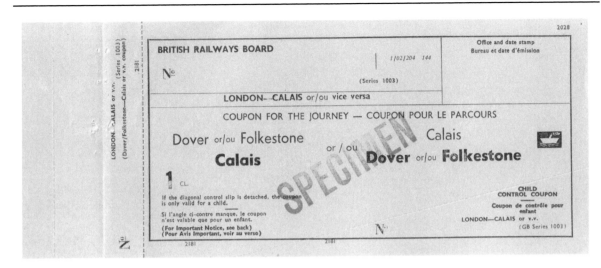

<115>

<116>

<117>

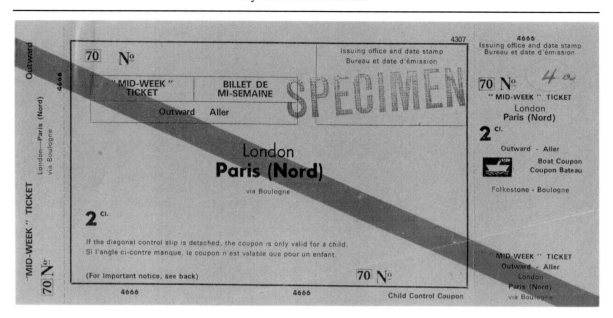

<118>

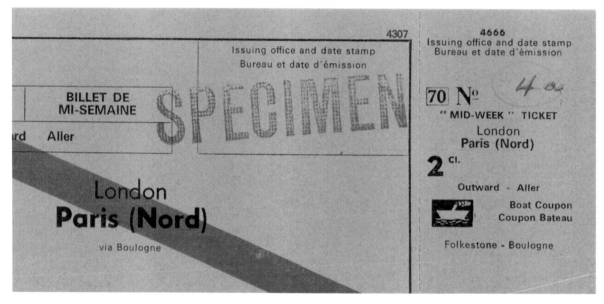

<119>

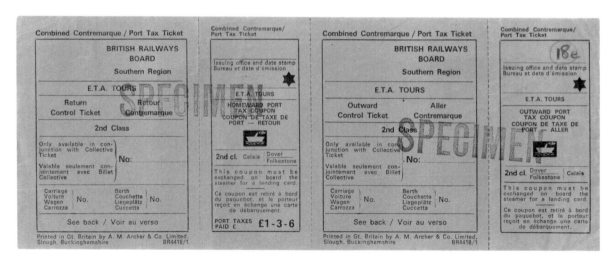

<120>

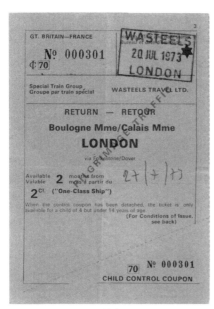

<123><123>
<124>

<122>

<123>

<125>

<126>

Seaspeed

In the mid 1960`s a new form of transport came into service in the shape of the hovercraft. Interestingly, British Railways saw the potential of this and set up a wholly owned subsidiary, British Rail Hovercraft Limited (and jointly with SNCF to operate services to France), which was marketed as "Seaspeed".

The limited company was established in 1965, under authority given to it by the British Railways Act 1963 and started its first service in 1966 across the Solent from Southampton to Cowes.

Later this was joined by Portsmouth to Ryde and Portsmouth to Cowes services. The Solent routes were transferred to Hovertravel in 1976.

Seaspeed also started a cross-Channel service from Dover to Calais and Boulogne-sur-Mer, France using SR-N4 hovercraft in August 1968. It was withdrawn in 2000.

Southampton to Cowes closed in 1976, Portsmouth to Cowes opened on 23rd March 1967 but was suspended on 29th September 1969. Portsmouth to Ryde opened on 1st April 1968 and is still operated by Hovertravel Ltd.

I have one ticket from the Solent operations, being half of an Ultimatic <127>, <128> which clearly defines British Rail Hovercraft Ltd as the operator. Ticket <129> is a paper issue from a pack, hand written on issue, for the Southampton to Cowes service. Ticket <130> actually defines that travel is by Hovercraft for the Boulogne to Dover section.

<127>

<128>

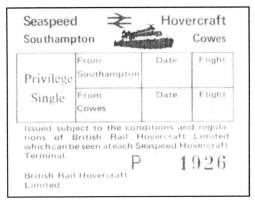

<129>

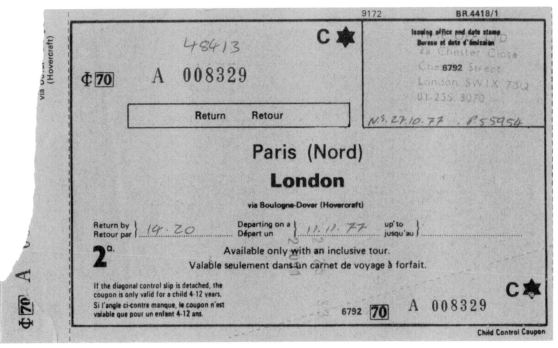

<130>

Jetfoil

Then for a short period in the 1960's there was yet another form of transport which BR also operated, in the shape of a jetfoil, in effect a hydrofoil craft powered by water jets. A boarding card from this operation is shown <131>, indicating the same involvement of the three operators as in <125> above but has wording in four languages.

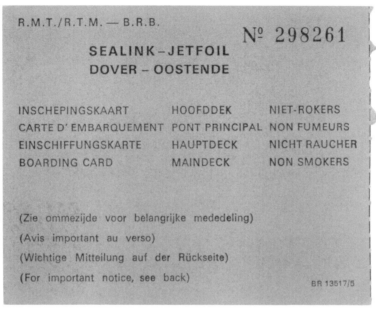

<131>

Toll Bridges

British Railways inherited ownership of a number of bridges for which tolls were levied. We have already crossed that at Barmouth but there were three others in the south east of England which produced many tickets. Initially these were of punch type, issued by Southern Railway and they continued into issues by BR but towards the end there were extensive ranges of Ultimatic tickets reflecting different categories of traffic crossing the toll.

Lymington <**132**>

A toll was charged for road access along the embankment to the railway station for which BR issued tickets in a style common to the other tolls nearby. I don't have an exact date when the toll was lifted but it is presumed to be contemporaneously with the others in the area.

<132>

Old Shoreham

The bridge carried the coastal trunk road - the A27 road - until 1970 when its successor was built a quarter mile to the north. The British Railways Board closed the rail service on 7th March 1966 but continued to collect tolls for road traffic until this was finally closed to road traffic on 7th December 1970. At the time the bridge closed it was the last public road bridge in Sussex to be controlled by a toll. There are extensive ranges of punches issued by BTC/BRB and eventually these were changed to Ultimatics of which a couple are illustrated here. <**133**>, <**134**>.

<133>

<134>

Brading <**135**>

Following earlier BTC issues, BRB Ultimatic issues for this toll causeway first appeared in 1966 before it passed into private hands in 1968.

<135>

The River Thames and North Sea

The Thames has always formed a formidable barrier to being crossed and ferries can trace a very long history, with that between Tilbury and Gravesend being no exception. BR found themselves owners of it in 1948 and ticketing practices were no different from that of their other operations. The vehicle ferry operation closed on 1st January 1965, when the Dartford Tunnel opened and the remaining foot passenger operation at Gravesend was transferred from the Town Pier to the erstwhile car ferry terminal (West End Pier) on 27th June 1965. Illustrated tickets depict these changes. <136>, <137>, <138>, <139>, <140>.

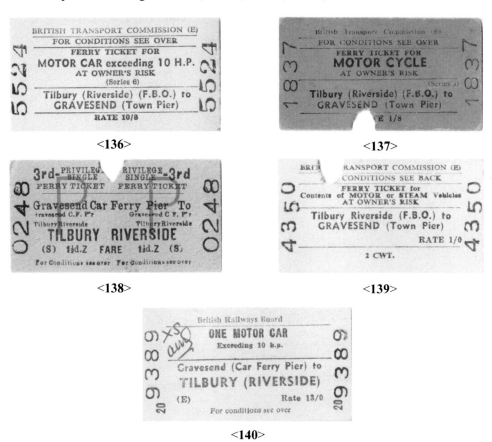

<136>   <137>

<138>   <139>

<140>

Tickets issued for this service routinely proclaim themselves as 'Ferry Tickets'.

A boat train also ran from Tilbury (Riverside) to St. Pancras in a similar manner to such services from Southampton, and a ticket from this service is illustrated. <141>.

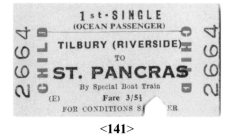

<141>

A very late addition to my collection, kindly given to me by the Editor of these addresses, is an Omniprinter, showing the Sealink UK Ltd title. As such, it is the only specimen from this machine used by BR for one of the ferry services that I am aware of. <142>.

<142>

River Humber

We now venture along the east coast to the River Humber. This is also a formidable crossing and the ferry had a long history.

Trams

However, before we cross it we encounter yet another form of transport which BR owned and operated , namely a tram system in the form of the Grimsby & Immingham Electric Railway, inherited from the London & North Eastern Railway (LNER). It ran on standard gauge track, with electrified tramway-style overhead and large single deck bogie tramcars but was not connected to the main railway network. The LNER issued an extensive range of punch tickets reflecting the operations. What is of particular note is that the tickets were entitled for the service. Both the titles and the types were continued by BTC and subsequently by BRB. The section from Grimsby to Cleveland Bridge closed on 1st July 1956 and the remainder continued until closure five years to the day in 1961. A selection of tickets is illustrated. <143>, <144>, <145>, <146>, <147>, <148>.

<143>

<144>

<145>

<146>

<147>

<148>

Humber

Victoria Pier on the Yorkshire coast at Kingston-upon- Hull was owned by the City Council and thus tolls were levied, although the ferries plying across to the Lincolnshire coast to New Holland pier were operated by BR. The usual and extensive range of 'standard' tickets was on issue <149>, <150>, <151>, <152>, <153>, <154>, <155>, <156>.   However the unusual feature here was a red overprint applied to those tickets for which the toll had been paid as part of the journey. This even extended to tickets issued 'on the spot' and a Multiprinter ticket is illustrated which includes said overprint, albeit not very accurately <157>.

<149>

<150>

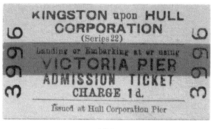

<151>

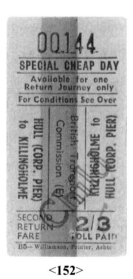

<152>

<153>

<154>

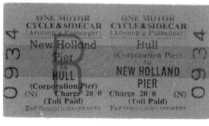

<155>

<156>

<157>

The longest suspension bridge in the world (at the time) was opened on 25th June 1981, upstream from Hull and the ferry ceased that day. Passengers thence had to make the journey across the river via the Humber Bridge which caused a degree of outrage at the time because it took longer than on the ferry. As the imminent end of the ferry drew nigh, BR promoted cruises from the Hull pier, and these included bus tours where Kingston-upon-Hull City Transport was involved. A selection of tickets from these operations are illustrated at <158>, <159>, <160>, <161> which also included sailing from Grimsby. A blue overprint was applied for private hire tolls.

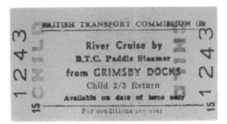

<158>

<159>

6889	6889
KINGSTON UPON HULL CITY TRANSPORT/ SEALINK (U.K.) LTD., INCLUSIVE TOUR	KINGSTON UPON HULL CITY TRANSPORT/ SEALINK (U.K.) LTD., INCLUSIVE TOUR
0923	0923
Kingston upon Hull Circular Bus Tour	**Hull (Corporation Pier) to New Holland and Back**
CHILD (5 to 13 years inclusive) №. 004507	CHILD (5 to 13 years inclusive) №. 004507
Date...........	TOLL PAID Date...........
Valid as Advertised	Valid as Advertised
Issued subject to byelaws and regulations of Kingston upon Hull Transport	Issued subject to the regulations and conditions in the publications and notices of the British Railways Board
Not Transferable	**Not Transferable**

(left margin vertical text: No. 004507   CHILD (5 to 13 yrs inc)   INCLUSIVE TOUR   0923)

<160>

BRITISH RAILWAYS BOARD (Z)	BRITISH RAILWAYS BOARD (Z)
BOOK N°. 00104 TICKET No. 10/02	BOOK N°. 00104 TICKET No. 10/01
SINGLE JOURNEY	SINGLE JOURNEY
ONE PASSENGER (Toll Paid)	**ONE PASSENGER** (Toll Paid)
Between **HULL CORPORATION PIER** and **NEW HOLLAND PIER** Available in either direction	Between **HULL CORPORATION PIER** and **NEW HOLLAND PIER** Available in either direction
Not available after	Not available after ....
CONDITIONS Issued subject to the Conditions and Regulations in the Board's Publications and Notices NOT TRANSFERABLE	CONDITIONS Issued subject to the Conditions and Regulations in the Board's Publications and Notices NOT TRANSFERABLE

<161>

North Sea

BR were involved in operating the ferries from Harwich across the North Sea to Hook of Holland. A typical journey would start by rail from London (Liverpool St) to Harwich, then by ferry to The Hook and thence onward to the Continent by rail. Even in this era the nature of the crossing was such that there were few, if any, foot passengers making just the ferry crossing. Thus ticketing was inevitably by issue of multi-coupon airline style tickets as illustrated <162>, <163>, <164> and <165>. Indeed I do not have any Edmondsons in my collection for just the Harwich-HoH crossing, unlike all the other crossings I have so far described, notably the English Channel.

<162>

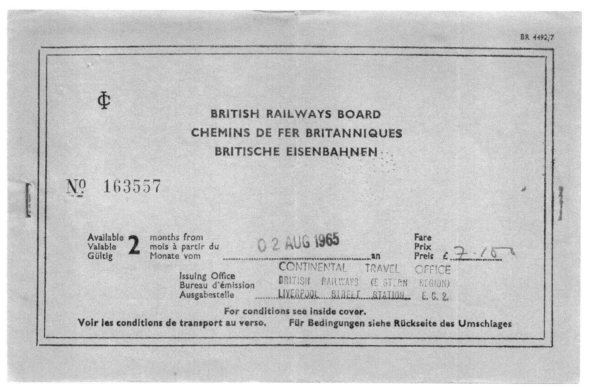

<163>

<164>

I conclude this eastern part of our journey by illustrating a multi-coupon ticket from Liverpool St to Hoek van Holland <165>. This incorporates a pictogram of an anchor to illustrate the shipping connection.

<165>

36

At this point I depict another two tickets:- London to Dieppe Mme via Newhaven Harbour <166>, and Calais Maritime to London via Dover/Folkestone <167> which are effectively in (and thereby indicating) the identical style of these tickets which was achieved in the early 1970's that the shipping division was now issuing.

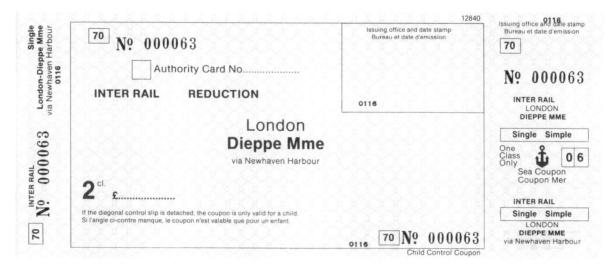

<166>

<167>

<168> and <169> are two control cards to attenuate disembarkation at Hook of Holland for passengers transferring to the onward, rail leg of their journey, via a number of named, 'through' services from London Liverpool Street.   The first is for the rail service from Hook of Holland via Utrecht and Hamburg to Copenhagen (arrival at 1900 hrs).   The second was for the rail journey to Basle which was introduced in 1952 to provide an additional daytime service to the established "Rheingold Express", albeit via a slightly different route in Germany.   At the request of British Railways this service was named in 1953 as the "Loreley Express".

<168>

<169>

Airports

Heathrow

Travelling to or from an airport by rail is not uncommon. Examples exist during the era of this address whereby it was possible to travel from an airport without any rail connection and be issued with a ticket issued by BR for a journey which necessitated using a bus for the first part. The major example was Heathrow airport where BR maintained a ticket office within the main terminal (as it was during the 1960's) and operated the so-called RailAir link services to High Wycombe, which later changed to Reading, and Feltham stations. Coaches were provided under contract initially by Rickards Coaches. It was entirely possible to travel just on the road journey and for which standard BR Edmondsons were issued. Ticket 0183 <**170**> takes us from a place we have already visited, namely Southampton, and by use of said link via another link, Woking, we arrive at Heathrow Air. Early tickets for the service from the airport had tickets showing the point of issue as London Airport and ticket 0223 <**171**> is for the service via High Wycombe, for which Rickards provided coaches. Later issues show the title as Heathrow Airport, for travel on the southwards link to Feltham <**172**> (with no specific operator shown), or the later, northwards, route to Reading, now provided by Alder Valley Coach <**173**>. Tickets <**174**>, <**175**>, <**176**>, <**177**> and <**178**> depict the changing styles of print on Edmondsons for the same journeys after decimalisation in February 1971.

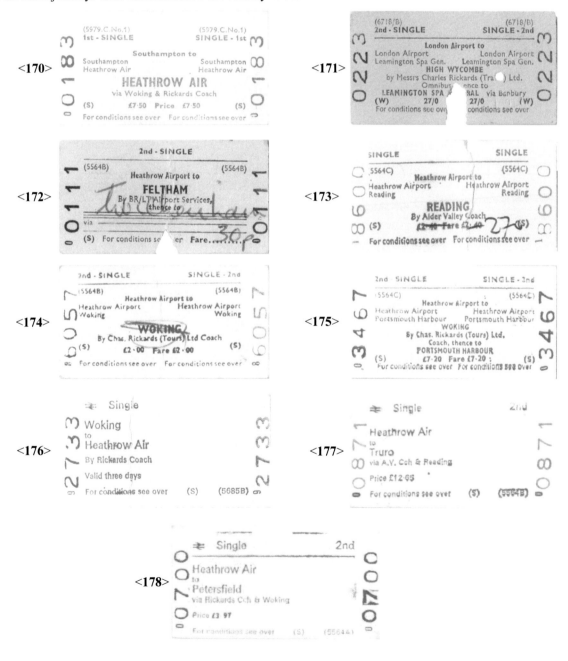

39

Luton

A similar facility was provided at this airport. Again, BR Edmondsons were issued from a terminal in the airport for initial road travel to the nearest station (Luton Flyer to Luton station). However examination of ticket 1775 <179> reveals a reference number BM12 which is believed to indicate that this ticket was issued by British Midland Airways as an agent for BR for passengers requiring transport to rail destinations. I digress from the remit of the address, to include another ticket style from the era, namely an INTIS, <180> and while this would start with a rail journey it depicts that the facility to travel to the airport as part of a rail journey was sufficiently busy to warrant blank stock being printed and held at other stations.

<179>

<180>

Southend

Likewise at Southend where it was possible to travel by bus between Rochford Station and the airport but be issued with Edmondson style tickets. Here the actual ticket <181> is issued from a Multiprinter, clearly showing it to be an Omnibus ticket. To note is that it is a single but is valid in either direction. The service was provided by Eastern National Omnibus Co. Ltd.

<181>

Buses

<182>, <183>, <184>, <185>, <186>, <187>, <188>, <189>, <190>, <191>, <192>, <193>, <194>, <195>, <196>, <197>, <198>, <199>, <200>, <201>, <202>

We are now in Yorkshire where BR found itself operating buses. The reason is long and complicated but the operations were inherited from previous arrangements with the London Midland & Scottish Railway (LMS) and LNER railway grouping companies. Essentially, in the early days of the 1930's four councils, who operated, inter-alia, buses outside the council territories, entered into arrangements with the railway companies so that the latter were enabled to operate buses in their own right but without infringement on the Council operations. To enable this they actually owned their own buses, identifiable as such within the respective Council fleets. Four Councils were involved, being Sheffield, Huddersfield, Halifax and Todmorden. For each operator, a Joint Operating Committee (JOC) was set up with the railway companies to oversee matters. BTC inherited the railway bus fleets on nationalisation and the arrangements continued through into BRB hands until the interests passed to the National Bus Company on 1st January 1969.

In all instances ticketing followed the practices of the Council but with separate sets of tickets which included reference to the JOC in the titles.

Note that each of the committees had their own titles:-

Halifax Joint Committee

Huddersfield Joint Omnibus Services

Sheffield Joint Omnibus Committee

Todmorden Joint Omnibus Committee

In Sheffield the buses which BR owned were actually allocated to a separate fleet designated as the 'C' fleet, although they were maintained as part of the Corporation fleet. The ticketing reflected this division of ownership and a selection of the very extensive number of them is illustrated.

A treasure within my collection is the Hall Autographic, clearly showing British Railways as one of the operators. Alongside are Ultimates, Setright Speeds and a TIM. Separate issues of Ultimates and Setrights had both Corporation and joint titles whereas TIMs always had the joint title.

The other three operators issued tickets in a similar manner and representative tickets from each are illustrated.

<182>, <183>, <184> Punch tickets of Todmorden JOC, and <185>, a Setright Speed.

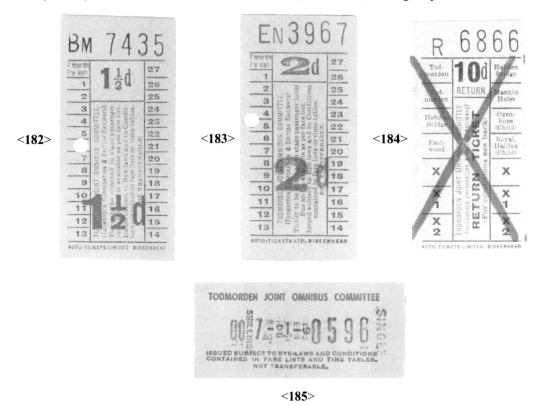

<185>

<186>, <187>, <188>. A Punch ticket from Huddersfield and Ultimates, with prefixed and suffixed serials.

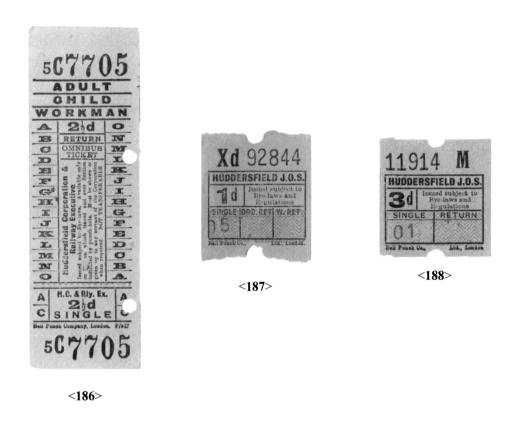

<187>

<188>

<186>

<189>, <190>, <191>, <192>. Punch tickets from Sheffield.

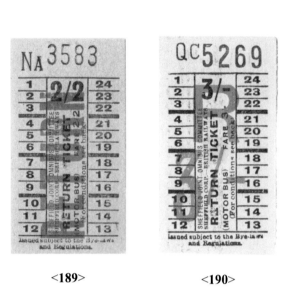

<189>   <190>   <192>

<191>

<193>, <194>, <195>, <196>, <197>, <198>. Ultimates from Sheffield.

<193>   <194>

<195>

<196>   <197>

<198>

<199> Hall Autographic, <200> TIM, <201> Setright Speed and <202> Bellgraphic from Sheffield.

<199>

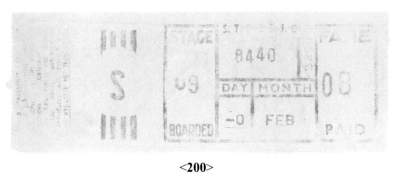

<200>

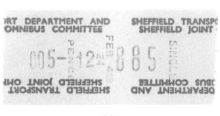

<201>

<202>

<203> Punch ticket and <204> TIM from Halifax.

<203>

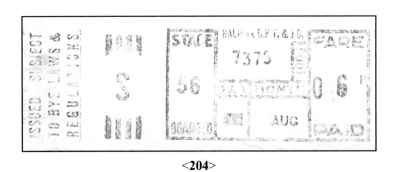

<204>

A feature of rail operations which has a long history is that of the bus exchange ticket. This facility, offered at many stations throughout the country, enabled a passenger with a return railway ticket to travel out by rail but return by bus if there wasn't a suitable train available. I have deliberately not included these bus exchange tickets within this address as the outward journey would have been by a rail service but then a special ticket would have been issued for the return journey by bus. However, I illustrate one such specimen because I have an excuse to do so. <205> is a typical bus exchange ticket, allowing the holder to return by bus from Golcar, two stops from Huddersfield on the line to Slaithwaite and which closed in 1968. On the reverse <206> is the key to why I have no problem at all in illustrating this ticket, as it clearly shows being available by Hansons or Huddersfield JOC. But I have just determined that a Huddersfield JOC bus could be one owned by BR. So there is every chance that this return journey could have been made on a bus owned by BR! QED. Note, that the title refers to 'Committee', despite the earlier comment about 'Services'.

<205>

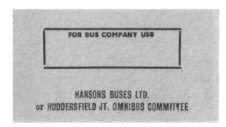

<206>

Scotland

We now move to Scotland. Arguments can be made for including tickets from <u>David MacBrayne Ltd</u> and the <u>Caledonian Steam Packet Co Ltd</u> because of their involvements at many and various times with the British Railways Board but these are complicated and tortuous. So I decided very early on to avoid them when putting this address together, although I acknowledge that there is a wealth of very interesting tickets available. I will relent though by illustrating a handful, not because of their travel content but to illustrate that BR also printed tickets for other operators. These are clearly in their print style. <**207**>, <**208**>, <**209**>, <**210**>, <**211**>, <**212**>, <**213**>, <**214**>.

<**207**>

<**208**>

<**209**>

<**210**>

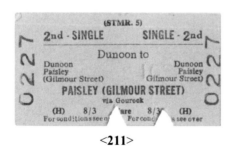

<**211**>

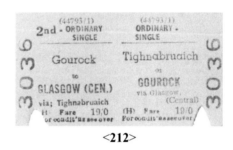

<**212**>

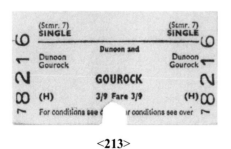

<**213**>

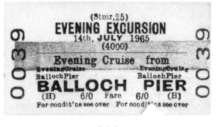

<**214**>

BR was responsible for two other two services in Scotland which didn't involve rail travel. For a while they were sole operators of the Kyleakin ferry from Kyle of Lochalsh to Kyleakin and illustrated is a punch ticket from that service <215>, <216>.

<215>

<216>

On yet another estuarial crossing, this time across the Falls of Lora at Connel Ferry the railway from Oban to Ballachulish crossed on a bridge of cantilever construction with a single line. There was sufficient space for a single carriageway of road alongside and, when trains weren't crossing, cars were allowed across on payment of a toll. Many different prints of punch tickets were produced, carrying on from pre-national days to BR issues. In latter days these were replaced by Ultimatics and typical specimens of both are illustrated <217>, <218>, <219>, <220>. The line to Ballachulish closed on 28th March 1966 and crossing the bridge by road vehicle then became toll free. Season tickets were issued, in standard BR style which progressively changed with time, and two are illustrated <221>, <222>.

<217> <218> <219> <220>

<221> <222>

Finale

Our excursion around the British mainland and to foreign ports is all but complete. However, there is one location still to be visited and this is the venue from which I obtained a certain ticket which I alluded to at the beginning. There have been cruise ships on Lake Windermere in the English Lake District since the early part of the 19th century and the railway companies were involved from their early days. BR inherited ownership of the operations together with the ships Swan, Swift, Teal and Tern, cruising from Ambleside to Bowness and Lakeside.

We were on holiday at Ambleside in 1964. We arrived at the booking office at Waterside to buy tickets for a cruise down the lake and back. Ambleside (as the pier was named) resembled a railway station, even to having totem nameplates, although it is of course many miles from a railway. There must be a special ticket for this I thought. But what was issued was totally unexpected to me, being as I said relatively new to ticket collecting. It was an Edmondson, in pure railway style. I was amazed. I noted as the cruise progressed that the crew assiduously collected the tickets as passengers disembarked. How on earth could I retain one? Dad was happy to be part of the plan. On our return to Ambleside, he and I went straight to the head of the queue, leaving Mum and my sister well back. We had our own tickets but when it came to our turn to get off Dad said "oh yes – my wife has our tickets – she's that lady back there" . "Oh ok" said the boatman and off we went – clutching tightly onto the tickets illustrated here <223>, <224>.

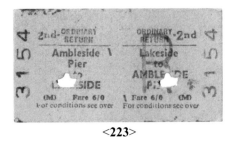
<223>

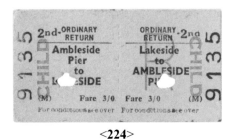
<224>

There were many types of tickets issued and I include an issue from Bowness <225> together with an Ultimatic <226> from the same pier for the sake of completeness.

<225>

<226>

From 10th May 1970 until 1973 Almex A's were used showing A for Ambleside, on green paper, B for Bowness on buff and L for Lakeside on green. Operations duly passed to Sealink in 1970 and when privatised in 1984 Stena marketed the service as the Windermere Iron Steamboat Co. In May 1993 it was sold to the local operator, Bowness Bay Boating Co. Ltd.

However the two Edmondsons I kept remain some of the most treasured tickets in my collection and to me form a fitting end to this address.

Thank you for travelling with me.

Appendix

TTS – Presidential Address – 2012 – By Bus & Boat on BR by Colin Page		
Tickets provided by Phil Drake		
Page	**Ref no.**	**Ticket serial no.**
5	13 & 14	0348 & 0821
6	18	0023
6	19	0347
8	26	0114
8	27	9999
9	31	8552
12	45	1709
14	58	2317
33	156	3666
34	158	1243
34	159	8911
39	177 & 178	0871 & 0700
47	215 & 216	27198
47	221	3256

Appendix